AF226139

Poetry's Might

Poetry's Might

Rhymes to Celebrate Life

RAPHAEL CANALI

RESOURCE *Publications* · Eugene, Oregon

POETRY'S MIGHT
Rhymes to Celebrate Life

Resource Publications
An Imprint of Wipf and Stock Publishers
199 W. 8th Ave., Suite 3
Eugene, OR 97401

www.wipfandstock.com

PAPERBACK ISBN: 978-1-6667-8607-1
HARDCOVER ISBN: 978-1-6667-8608-8
EBOOK ISBN: 978-1-6667-8609-5

Poetry's might: Rhymes to celebrate life
Published By Raphael Canali

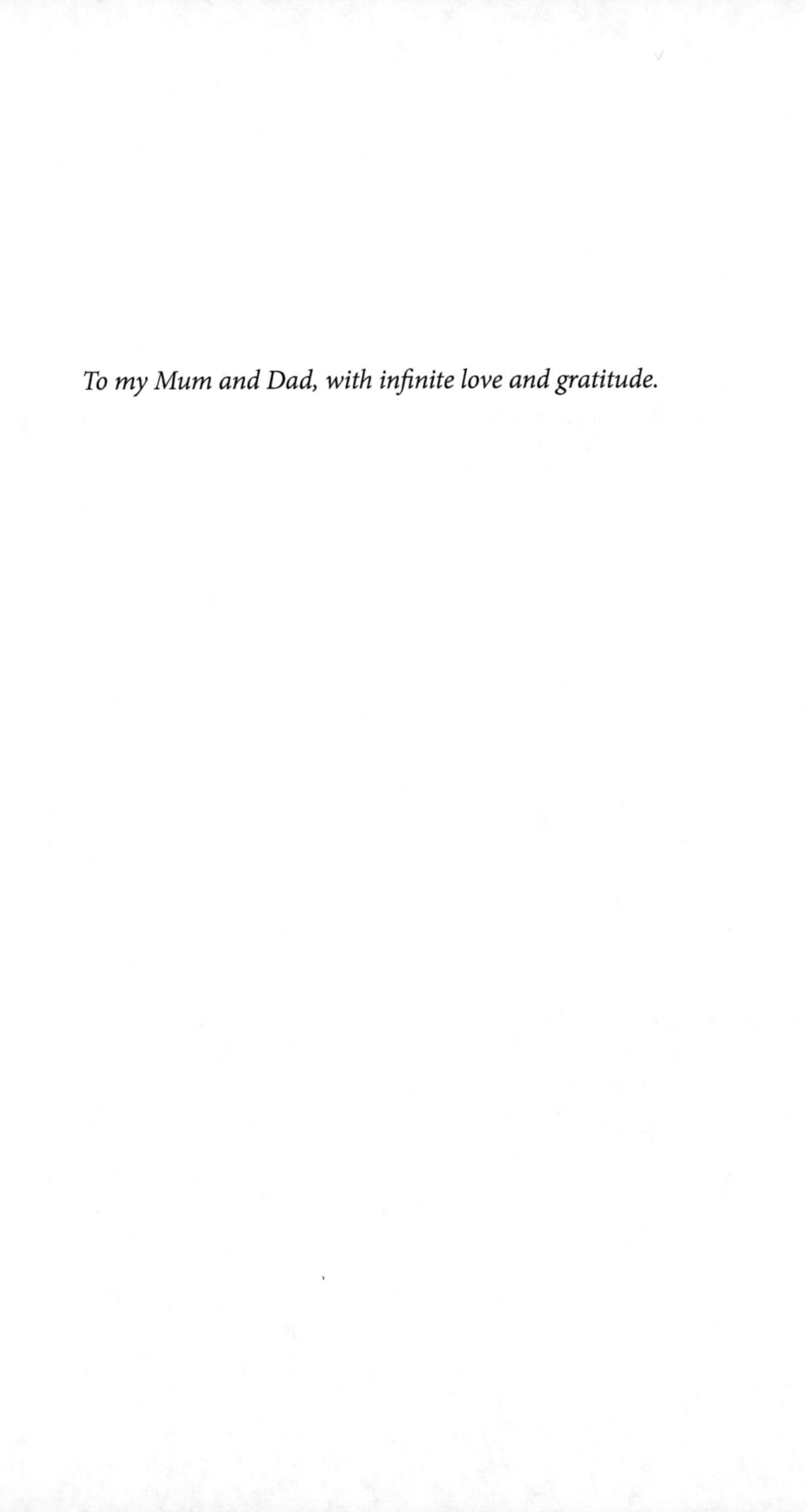

To my Mum and Dad, with infinite love and gratitude.

Always remember that you are absolutely unique.
Just like everyone else.

—MARGARET MEAD

Contents

Contents

THE WALK IN A WINTER NIGHT

Walking in the dark, calm night
Smiling back at the stars' might
While the trees hum their own melody
And the snowflakes warm your heart's ecstasy.

Soil, plants, cars, and much more
Frozen to their core
And closed windows fighting
Coldness roar.

You however walk through the peace of night,
And your flaming and warm hope's light
Gives a second life
To your surrounding frozen sight.

Uncountable souls
You meet every day.
On the streets, in the books, on the screen
You see their faces.

But in a matter of a second,
You forget their life.
Dancing through your own day,
Their presence no more in your life's play.

However, when I met
your glance,
My heart only for you
Danced.

For an infinite second,
You made time stop,
While the beauty of your smile
Made me feel the rush of its ecstasy.

You,
I'll never forget.

THE MIND

Universal in its
Existence,
Unique to
Life's essence.

Offering millions
Of opportunities,
For the shining of
Our own being.

It is the key to
Our acceptance.
Love it. Celebrate it.
For yourself, be its saviour.

TIME FOR A COFFEE, NOT FOR A CALL

Sitting in a Parisian bar,
Sunglasses and a cigar.
Enjoying the warm delight
Of the sun's bright light.

Sipping on a ten-dollar coffee,
For a full hour
Complaining to a friend,
No time to call his mother.

Busy pretending to be someone he isn't,
Appearance over life's essence,
He forgot who made it possible for him
To sit there.

What a sad counterplot.

ART

Celebrating the beauty
Of life,
It accepts all form of expression
With great delight.

Judging it does not
At all,
Welcoming every single one
Of humanity's soul.

Feel free to express
Life's harmony
While waltzing with
Your soul's creativity.

Art is life.
Life is art.

THE MADMAN WHO ESCAPED THE PSYCH WARD

As his sadness wanes away
And the sun's warm light
Caresses his skin,
He welcomes the beautiful charm of craziness
On the hills of life's lightness.

He smiles.
He laughs.
He rolls in the grass
And flies with hope.

For long minutes,
Before, mindcuffed away,
He laughed at his mind's
Prison maker.

For a second there,
All in his mind,
Free as he can,
He won.

He for long considered it a curse.
Day and night
fighting its might.
He asks himself, why me?

But one day he cried. "Nonsense",
What if it is part of the way.
Nobody escapes its grip,
Maybe he understood its gift.

It makes you understand
Life's gift he said.
And will lead you to the better tomorrow's
Lift.

Trying times may not be there
Forever.
But what you'll learn from it
Makes it worth it.

THE LONELY BILLIONAIRE

As you kiss your partner good night,
In his lost delusions
He kisses his liquor's
Long night.

Blinded by the money
He always wanted,
He now longs for a simple hug
While all he has is an endless chug.

Raging under the night's dancing stars,
He would give everything for a loving smile.
But as he takes his eighteenth sip,
He remembers choosing money over love's gift.

Priorities.
Priorities.
Priorities.

Think freely,
Take the boulevards of life's unknowns
And while you do so
Make sure to thank your soul.

Use the beauty of your spirit,
Wherever. However,
In your inner self
You'll have to dig for it.

Whatever troubles
Cloud your way,
Trust it,
It is your guard.

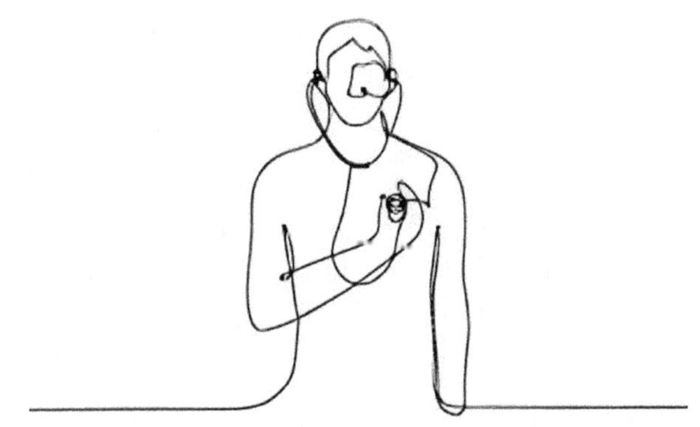

THE POISON OF THE PESSIMISTS

They lose each second
Without reason.
Against themselves,
They commit treason.

Ignoring the beauty in each day's life,
They forget death's coming whip.
Having forgotten their true being,
Salvation in their heart no longer humming.

When life to end arrives,
They realise to late they've never been living.
As they pray for a second chance
Smiling death's kiss takes them for a dance.

THE CLOCK

Tic tac
Goes the clock.

Bright and dark
Goes your hope.

Happy and sad
You dance with love.

One question remains.

Where will you go?

THE BEACH, THE BEER, THE FRIENDS

What a beautiful Night
For these young souls
Enjoying life's light.

Celebrating friendship
On the cold nightly sand,
Their love and story
Makes it a warm and welcoming land.

To what was,
To what is,
To what will be,
With them, let's all raise our beers.

THE BEAUTY OF LIFE CAN BE A TRAGEDY

You live without knowing
Why or how it all happened
And you die not knowing
What after, will come for you.

Embrace the scariness
Of these question's black hole
And stroll
In the midst of it all.

However miss it,
Scared.
Oh, that
You will regret.

LOVING HEART, LOVE'S RIGHT

Whoever you might be,
Whatever people told you to be,
Be yourself, proud and strong
And break hate's wall.

Love is a human right,
A universal right,
Protect your own heart.
Trust it, it'll be alright.

THE GREAT GREY SUIT OF MY GREAT GRANDPA

It travelled the world,
Through Asia, Africa,
And the rest of it all,
With each of their styled aroma it rode.

Giving him the elegance
Of the young man he always was
I still can smell the scent
Of his Cuban cigars
That accompanied it all.

For now, breezed everyday
In my barn's bay,
It's last adventure
It has not played.

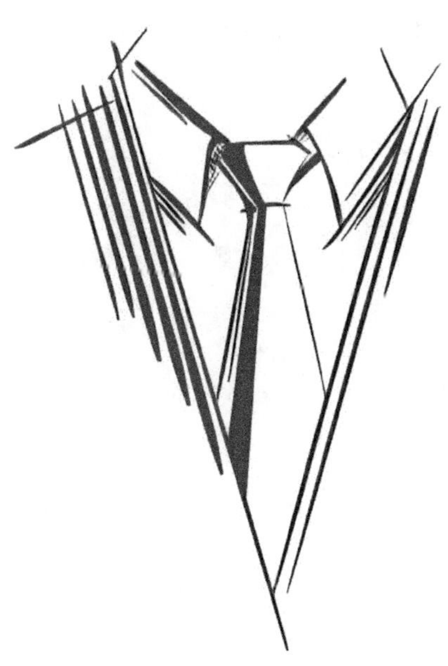

THE STEW OF YOUR OWN THOUGHTS

Like a melody
In a film
And a brush
On a painting

It gives
Your soul
Its essence.
Shining.

Chose the note carefully,
Brush the colour lovingly,
And on the road of its guidance,
Dream endlessly.

THE HEALTHY PLANT AND ITS OPTIMISTIC DANCE

On a Sunday Evening,
Like every single day,
Lilly the plant wakes up
To the boulevard's ballet.

Today however the dances,
Gone.
Replaced by the angry faces' decay.
It rains.

Lilly however smiled
As the rain feeds her reign.
His owner happy too,
Lilly will live to see another day.

Both enjoying the calmness
Of the rain,
They, each in their way
Prepare for tomorrows new play.

JUST FUCKING GO

Tic tac
Time to go.
All your fears
Have to go.

Why worry about
What could go wrong
If every experience you have
Feeds your life's song.

Make it a ballet
Not a macabre play.
Dance with the stars
And enjoy your day.

THE PAST

Look through the future,
Not via its past.
True to yourself,
Follow your path.

The past is no more
Your concern.
Hold on to it
And you'll forget to live.

THE FUTURE

What will tomorrow
Give us to follow?
Stand proud and tall
Dance in the unknown.

Trust it all.
For future
For you and I
Is where we'll rise.

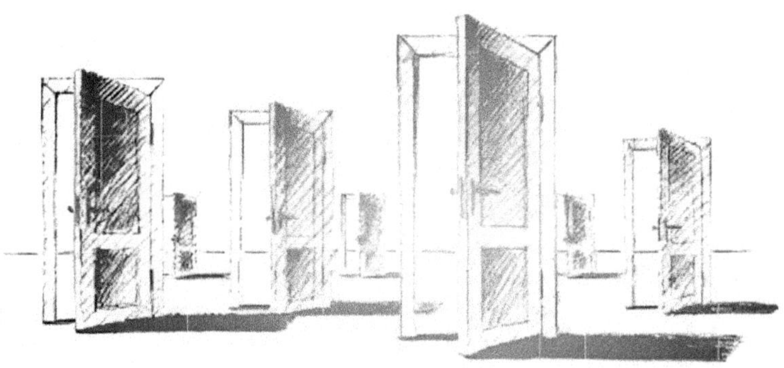

ODDS

What if,
What after,
You believed,
You became your spark.

Roll the dice.

TIME

Time, like fire
Or love's banter
Consumes your
Heart's Sapphire.

So, through that fire
Dance with laughter
And to the approaching sound
Of death's sonata

Show it with proudness,
You're the rhythm master.

THE BEAUTY OF GRIEF

Between the tears
And screams,
Your soul aching
Crushed by loss' fear.

On that grey gravestone,
Where time passes
Without any milestone,
You are here.

You are here to grow,
You are here to remember.
Sometimes tears draw a smile,
Knowing souvenirs never die.

That casket
Underground
Forever sealed
Your memories around.

Smile for what was,
Thank your god,
But always know,
You'll meet again.

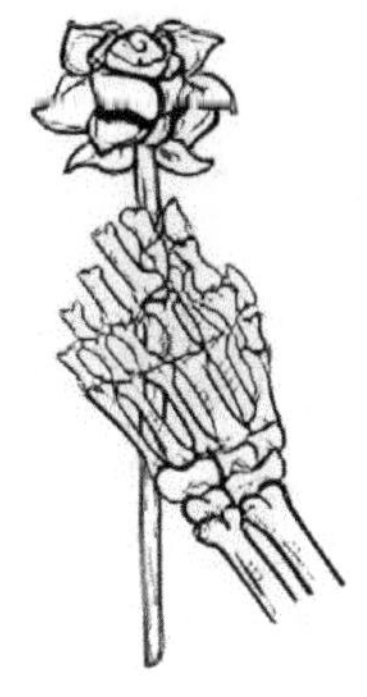

STRANGER LOVER

Do you realize
That
Without ever knowing you
Still every day I miss you.

Do you realize
That
Without ever seeing you,
Always, I'll love you.

MADNESS INVITATION

A Pinch of
Madness.
A Spark
Of life.

Where madness
Comes,
The Spirits
Roar.

Long live our
Madness,
For the past, present
And life as a whole.

THE MAN AND HIS WINTER GUITAR

While crisp white snowflakes
Illuminate our space,
On a cold winter night
The angels hear one of life's delights.

Between giant
Mountain rows,
Inside a humble wooden home,
Melody's fire roars.

Illuminating the calm night's Tune,
His guitar strings
Guided by nature's quiet symphony.

Each finger movement proudly
Celebrates joy's ability.
While he embraces creativity,
Nature goes into that night. Gently.

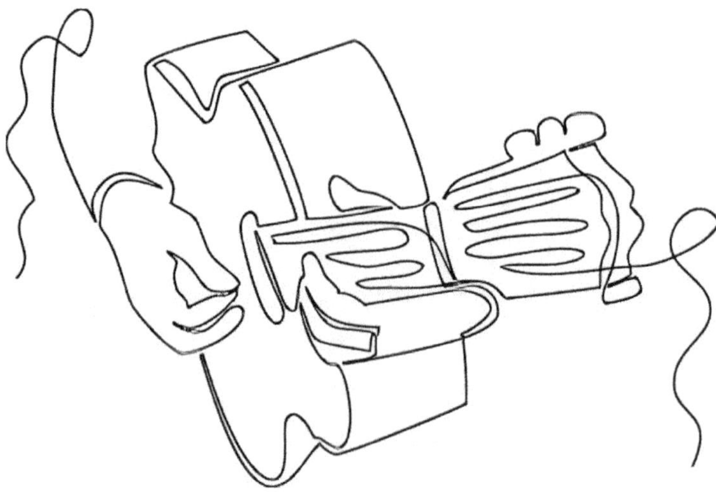

THE HALF-EMPTIED BEER BOTTLE

Sitting on the cold sand,
On a cool night,
With rare stars
Shining their light.

What does it hold?
More than just beer.
Secrets, sadness, joy.
Life's musketeer.

Here comes the stray cat,
Lost in the night.
By the power of his tail,
He spills that beer's tale.

TIME FLIES

You don't see it
coming
But before your eyes
It happens.

Invisible to our
Sight,
Consuming
Our life.

No one escapes
Its invisible grip,
So you might as well
Make the most of it.

Are you too
Afraid to
Get
Older?

NOSTALGIA

This pang in the
Heart.
Mixed feeling
Of sadness and life's rise.

Comforting for your
Past,
Challenging for your future's
Bypass.

Oh nostalgia,
When you hold us.

DON'T PUSH

I was walking towards
My plane
When I saw that red button say:
"Don't push".

Startled by the enormity of the irony,
A big red button on a plane's blue wall
Asking to us all
Not to be touched.

I didn't intend to push it
But that, it's just asking
For it.
Who even chose the colours?

It looked at me
With its glooming red
Stare.
Oh, he wanted to play that game.

What could it possibly do,
This fat red button
Lost in meters of blue.
Is it to call the painter
And argue?

Oh god,
I'm gonna miss my flight,
That red button sure knows
How to fight.

AND THAT WAS HIS HOME

A small cabin
In the woods,
Covered in snow
Majestic it looks.

Simple furniture,
Beautiful?
Years of usage
Still a new soul.

On the warm chimney
A photo of his wife.
Looking upon the cabin,
Watching wise.

Cosy warmth between
His walls.
Throughout the years
Their love still calls.

Between the trees
Of the woods,
That cabin has its world
Of its own.

That was his home.

THE DANCING TODDLER IN THE MORNING

Out of his crib,
Feeling sun's rift,
She dances
On her small feet.

Did she feel good
Because of the sun?
One thing is sure
She wasn't alone.

She, herself, and joy,
Dreaming in fun
Maybe she just felt good,
She was alive just like the sun.

BROTHER AND SISTER

No matter
How much they fought.
They still loved
Each other's love thought.

No matter the
Anger,
Love
Always conquered.

For the rest of
Their life,
Together
They'll fight.

LOST RULES

What becomes of rules
If no one follows them?
What are orders
If no onYe obeys?

Freedom or chaos?
Maybe both.
Let's see
What happens.

Just like apples
In the store,
People try
To choose the best of them all.

Just like the apple
In your bowl,
It will help you
Or it will sicken you.

Choose your apples wisely.

VIRTUAL LOVE MESSAGE

I Love you so much.
Sent he to her.

Sorry, not delivered.
Said phone to him.

You never say
You love me
Said her to he,
Before saying: "it's over".

Phone's rigidity beats love's fragility.

DREAM ON

The beauty of love
Makes me tear down.
The beauty of life
Makes me dream on.

WINTER BREEZE

In the snowy streets,
Between the sweet breeze,
White houses, and trees
Snow embraces everything.

Between the snowflakes
Of sweet cold time,
Christmas spirit
With our heart rimes.

It may feel cold
On the outside
But the warmth of the period
Heats you from the inside.

I love snow.

THE FRAGILITY OF LIFE

A bullet,
A knife
A stroke
Much more
Can end It all.

Protect it,
Enjoy it,
Love it,
Enjoy it.

You have
One shot
At
It.

Never stop
Believing.
Never stop
Dreaming.